My
Mornington Peninsula
Adventure
Belongs to:

Look out for Nelly The Wombat
.....she likes to hide!

For Harry and for Jacob

Harry loves 'writing' letters to his Grandparents known as Mac and Pa.
'My Mornington Peninsula Adventure' is another letter Harry wishes to
share with you as part of the 'My Adventure Series'.

This series has been created to promote Australia.
More important however, it is to encourage children
to have a sense of fun and imagination.
We also hope that children will be
encouraged to write a letter....and post it!

Look out for further books in this series:

Published by Rothwell Publishing
9 Clarke Avenue Warburton, Victoria, Australia, 3799
www.rothwellpublishing.com
rothwellpublishing@bigpond.com
Tele: 61 3 5966 5628

First Published 2006
Reprinted 2009
Text copyright ° Jo Rothwell 2006
Illustrations copyright ° Bryce Rothwell 2006

Typeset by Artastic Images
Printed in China by Everbest Printing Co. Ltd

National Library of Australia Cataloguing-in-Publication data:

Rothwell, Jo, 1962-.
My Mornington Peninsula Adventure..

For children.
ISBN 0 9757230 2 2.

1. Mornington Peninsula (VIC.) - Juvenile fiction. I. Rothwell, Bryce, 1966-. II. Title.

A823.4

My Mornington Peninsula Adventure

Jo Rothwell
Illustrated by
Bryce Rothwell

Rothwell
Publishing

Dear Mac and Pa,
How are you today?
The weather is fine on our beach holiday.
We had an adventure, Nelly and me,
At Mornington Peninsula ....read on and you'll see.

Mummy and Daddy, Nelly and I,
Were sculpting sand on the foreshore at Rye.
I built a sand creature with seaweed for hair,
Shells for his mouth, his nose and his stare.

An odd thing occurred when I stood back to look,
The leg on my sand beast wiggled and shook.
It opened its mouth, said 'G'day, name is Clive',
I'd created a sand monster, and now it's **alive!**

Pandemonium! Everyone scattered in fright.
Clive shuffled to the left.... and then to the right.
I ran and I hid, but he joined in the chase,
He followed close by with a grin on his face.

So........

I located a rod and a bucket of bait,
And a box of hooks, and then sat on a crate.

I pretended to fish on the jetty for whiting,
But Clive tagged along to ask what was biting.

I hid with the campers at Rosebud foreshore,
With tents and thongs and barbies galore.
I joined with a group who were playing beach cricket,
Slogging bat onto ball with a boogie-board wicket.

I thought I was safe from my sand beast creation,
Until Clive came to umpire this beach recreation.

Up Arthurs Seat, I rode in a chair,
I couldn't see Clive, but saw everywhere.
This view was amazing of Port Phillip Bay,
I liked it so much I could ride here all day.

But my joy disappeared when the chair came to stop,
For Clive was there helping folks off at the top.

I ran about here and I ran about there,
And ran into a maze and didn't know where.
I looked and I looked for the path to get out,
I was lost in this maze, so I started to shout.

I heard a voice call, 'What's all this rumpus?'
It was sand creature Clive standing there with his compass.

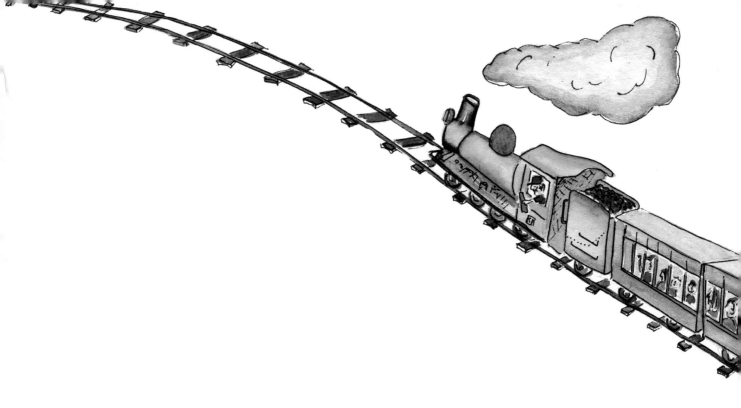

The steam train was waiting at Mornington station,
With train travellers ready in anticipation.
The guard signalled his flag, we were off down the track.
I sat back to listen ......clickety clack.

I was free from my sandy creation at last,.......
Until sand trickled down,....I sat shocked and aghast,
I looked up to the rack; I was no longer free,
It was Clive smiling down saying, 'Hello, Tickets Please'.

I dodged and I darted round Westernport Bay,
To find a place Clive would *not* come to play.
At the Point Leo Life Saving Carnival parade.
I held onto the rope and joined the brigade.

As a Nipper Life Saver I was feeling quite special,
With a hat and a rope and a floatation vessel.
We practiced life saving and I reeled in the line,
It was Clive on the end looking perfectly fine.

I raced off past Flinders to Bushrangers Bay,
It was here at Cape Schanck I would lead Clive astray.
The boardwalk descends to the edge of Bass Strait,
Where Pulpit Rock stands like a strong iron gate.

As waves crashed to shore I thought finally....at last,
Clive would not follow me down on this pass.
I hid among tea tree, I was quiet as a mouse.........But
Clive saw me and waved from the Cape Schanck Lighthouse.

Now Point Nepean was great to discover,
For this was the place I could hide and take cover,
Along tracks and in tunnels I could quickly escape,
In the old army section at the end of the cape.

I hid there for ages…..well at least thirty seconds,
When Corporal Clive found me, he silently beckoned.
Then bellowed 'Young soldier, you need to improve,
Your camouflage is no use if you fidget and move.'

I boarded a boat from the old Portsea pier.
And hid among divers checking their gear.
With goggles and flippers and floaties for me,
We chugged off to look at the stuff in the sea.

I saw twenty two dolphins alongside our boat,
They were guiding a skier in a bright yellow coat.
On closer inspection I saw it was Clive,
He had on a wet suit and was ready to dive.

I ran to the ferry at the end of the dock,
It left every hour, right on the dot.
We would journey to Queenscliff and return straight away,
Now this was a great way to fill in a day.

The loud speaker crackled, it hissed and it spluttered.
'Your Captain will speak now,' a crewmember muttered.
It was Captain Clive, who came on to say,
'Welcome aboard folk and have a nice day.'

So........

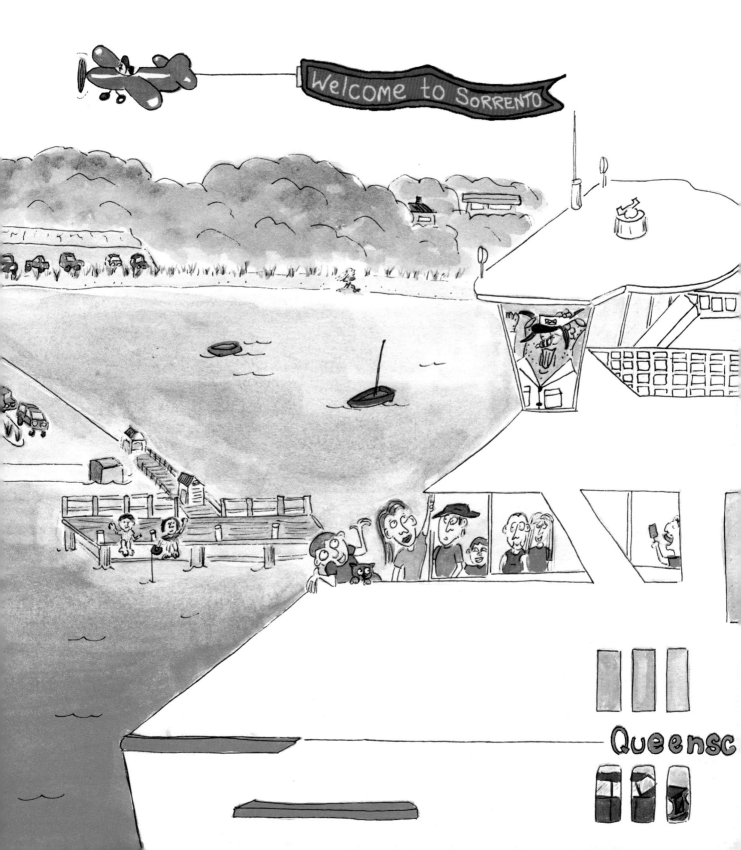

I returned to Rye, where all this began,
I knew what to do now, I had a great plan.
I dug in the sand with my bucket and spade,
I worked really hard, you should see what I made.

My sand creature family was finally complete,
With Clifford and Clancy and old Uncle Pete.
And Chloe and Claude who were wanting a brother,
Yes of course this was Clive,.....could there be any other?

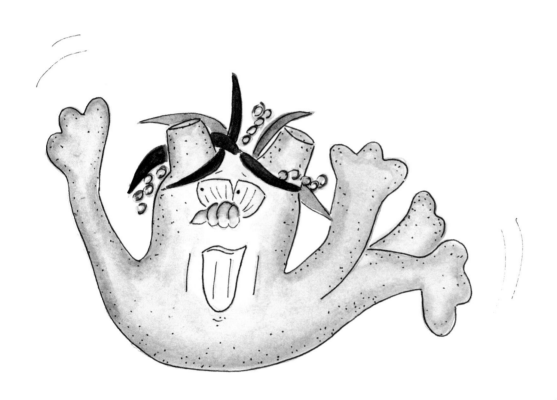

So........The chase was over, at last I was free,
For Clive was now chasing his new family!

Our time at Mornington Peninsula had come to an end,
And so is this letter I'll soon have to send.
I know we'll return, we will often come back,
And you can come too, Pa and Mac.

Love Always
Harry XXX

Rye Sand Sculpting

Did you know that tons of work goes into making a great sand sculpture? Sculptures use special sand like the sand used on building sites because each grain is square and it sticks together better. The beach sand grains are rounder so can fall down. Maybe this is why my sand castles don't last long. But that's okay because I get to build a new one each day.

Mazes

There seems to be lots of mazes to get lost in around here. I know that I have been to three mazes and all are amazing. I think it is really funny when Daddy gets lost and Mummy and I have to go and find him. Mummy says Daddy would get lost in our own back yard. I think this might have actually happened!

Rosebud Foreshore Camping

Mummy says that camping right on the beach is a tradition that lots of people love to do. I think this would be great because they don't have to walk for ages in the hot sun carrying towels and boats and boogie boards and buckets and spades and umbrellas and balls and fishing rods and floaties, and paddles and food and drink. And when it's time to go home after swimming they don't have to walk in the hot sun carrying towels and boats and boogie boards and buckets and spades and umbrellas and balls and fishing rods and floaties and paddles and left over sandy sandwiches!

Arthurs Seat Chairlift

Daddy says that the chairlift opened in 1960 which is nearly 50 years ago! On a clear day you might see You Yang Ranges, Dandenong Ranges, Cape Otway, and Mt Donna Buang. Now this is really exciting because Mt Donna Buang is just near where I live at Warburton. Daddy said he doesn't know if the chairlift will always be running but said it is such an icon of the Mornington Peninsula that we still wanted it in this book.

Mornington Steam Railway

Gosh I just love steam trains! I have been on lots and lots of steam train trips and the one from Moorooduc to Mornington is one of the best. Lots of people who also love trains help out so everyone can go for a ride. If you are really lucky you might get to go in the drivers cab! I can't wait till I go again…. neither can Mummy.

Cape Schanck Lighthouse

We had such a great time doing the lighthouse tour. Janet was our guide and told us all about the lighthouse and how important it was to save ships from crashing into rocks. The lighthouse has been here since 1859 and is one of the few left still operating. We went on the boardwalk to look at Pulpit Rock. It was a great walk but Daddy had to push Mummy up the steps on the way back. You can also walk to Bushrangers Bay. Mummy said it was called this because a long time ago there were two bushrangers Bradley and O'Connor. They escaped from goal in Tasmania and sailed across Bass Strait and this is where they came to shore.

Sorrento to Queenscliff Ferry

Now I just love going on this ferry. It goes from Sorrento to Queenscliff and then back again. You can walk on or drive your car on it and then get out of your car and then walk about. Most times we are running really late so have to run down the pier but we always manage to catch it. We have even taken our dogs BJ and Maibee on it. They love it too, except they are not allowed inside. That's okay because then you get to stay outside and look out for dolphins. I have seen so many dolphins swimming along side this ferry. WOW!

Point Nepean

This is a National Park and of course that means Daddy gets really excited. What I thought was so exciting was the tractor train thingy you get to ride in all the way to the end of the point. There are lots of old forts and tunnels and army stuff. This used to be an important place that army dudes lived to watch the sea because to get into Melbourne by boat, you have to go past the end bit here. It really doesn't look very far to the land across at Queenscliff. Mummy said that this is called the Heads and there is a really big Rip in the water. One time my teddy bear called Walter got a rip on its ear and Mummy sewed it up. I went here with Mac and Pa once and Pa told me he used to live here when he was a soldier. There are stacks of walks to do and I want to come back here again.

Point Leo Life Saving

Mummy said that the Point Leo Life Saving Club has been around since 1955. She remembers camping at Shoreham and used to go to some of the Life Saving Carnivals in the 1970's. Gosh she must be old! How great would it be to be a Nipper? A Nipper is just like the real grown up life saver only younger like me. You get to learn all these great skills and stuff.

First Settlement Site 1803

Did you know that even before people found Melbourne, they found Sorrento? Sorrento was the place that people from Europe first came to live in Victoria. Mummy said that indigenous people however have lived here for thousands of years.

Other Stuff

There is other stuff to do here too. You can go to The Briars Historic Park, Coolart Wetlands and Homestead, French Island, McCrae Homestead, and so much more. I think it's all great, but best is all the beaches along Western Port Bay and Port Phillip Bay.